Raising Child
Prodigies

Raising Child Prodigies

Jet Tiraphatna

Library of Congress Control Number:		2011911748
ISBN:	Hardcover	978-1-4628-9573-1
	Softcover	978-1-4628-9572-4
	Ebook	978-1-4628-9574-8

This book was printed in the United States of America.

To order additional copies of this book, contact:
Xlibris Corporation
1-888-795-4274
www.Xlibris.com
Orders@Xlibris.com
85327

CONTENTS

DEDICATION

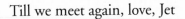

In loving memory of my Scoutmaster Robert Lee Squires who has always believed in me. The words, "You boys are doing a fine job, a fine job" could be heard during Scout meetings and on Scout outings. Some of my philosophy that I share in this book, I have picked up from Bob during our many late night campfire conversations. Through tough love and unconditional love, Bob has been a great leader, a guide, and a mentor to me. The Lord has blessed me by sending Bob to me. Well, Bob, you have done a fine job, a very fine job.

Till we meet again, love, Jet

ACKNOWLEDGEMENTS

First and foremost, I am thankful for God for all that He has done for me. I have felt His inspiration and guidance with this book.

To my wife and best friend, Chenda, who is an equal partner in raising and educating our five lovely children. She is encouraging and supportive of this and many of my "projects."

As writing is not my strong point, I am grateful to all of my editors and proof readers. My main editor is Professor Sherri Hodges of Cossatot Community College. Sherri was a wonderful English Professor for both Chendara and Marcie. Dwight D. Mendenhall, Dr. Robert Taylor, Dr. Sterling Lacy, Chendara, and Marcie contributed to the editing.

I am deeply appreciative to the fine institution at Cossatot Community College. They have truly opened their doors to us. The administration, instructors, and support staff has been very friendly. Milton Higginbotcham and Jill Turner were as enthusiastic as we were registering Chendara.

Thanks to my old friend Dr. Wayne E. Wright with University of Texas, San Antonio for advising me to create Part IV, "A Case for Child Prodigy."

Special thanks to David Molts with *Inside Higher Ed* for his professional journalism. Please see Appendix B. Thanks for the permission to reprint the entire article.

My gratitude goes to all of my friends, relatives, educators, and church leaders that believed in me. I also want to express my heartfelt gratitude and love of my country—USA. This truly is the bless land of opportunity. Again, for God, "With God, ALL Things are Possible."

INTRODUCTION

This is not a step-by-step book. Each child is different and we shouldn't use a cookie cutter to make them all the same. Even our identical twin boys are very different. This is not an end-all-be-all book. You may want to pick and choose from this book to individualize it for your child. This book is broken up into four parts. Part one is Philosophy & Principles. Part two is Program, Activities, and Games. Part three is College Admissions & Preparations. Part four is Making a Case for Child Prodigy. All four parts were based on personal research and experience.

Raising five children on limited budget left us no choice but to have them registered in public school. We did not have time to home school because we required a two parent income. In addition, public and private school is good for learning social skills. We believed in the myth that homeschooled children are not sociable. Since we could not afford private school, we made the best of the situation. With no formal child development degree or expertise, we developed our own philosophies and training.

Raising a prodigy child is not everything, nor is it the only thing. Children also need a good balance of physical, spiritual, and moral health. Will our society be better off if everyone is well educated? There are countless examples of

> *"For wisdom is better than rubies; and all the things that may be desired are not to be compared to it."*
>
> *Proverbs 8:11*

unethical business practices, corrupt governments, and evil geniuses. The Nazi doctors at Auschwitz and Dachau conducted human experiments and horrible crimes. Yet, no one will deny the intelligence of these doctors. Indeed, our children need great education coupled with great ethics. It is better to raise wise kids than smart kids.

America is truly a land of opportunity. After finishing nursing school in Thailand, my mom received a visa to come to America with my father. My mother has no higher education than her Registered Nurse (RN) degree, and my father has some college from Thailand. Their belief in education was strong and firm. Both of my sisters heeded to their educational counsel and graduated from USC and UCLA.

I was the black sheep of the family and did poorly in school. I remember my mom found my poor report card from junior high which was comprised of a "D" and an "F". I was kicked against the kitchen stove and fell to the ground. While I sat on the floor, she then proceeded to say, "I worked hard to bring our family to America so that you could go to school here. Many people in Thailand would give up so much to have the opportunity that you have. Do you know where you would be if you were still in Thailand? You could be anything you want and do anything with an education." Normally I would hear Charlie Brown in *Peanuts*, "wha-wha,wha,wha." Or today's Bart Simpsons in *The Simpsons*, "bla-bla,bla-bla." This time, I did pay attention, thought about what she said, and started taking education seriously. I had to work hard because of poor study habits. I did manage to finish community college and California State University, Long Beach. To this day, I am forever grateful for my mom for bringing us to America and putting me between the stove and her foot.

I am so glad that I didn't have to raise any children that were like me. We were blessed that our children love learning. When children are instilled with the passion for learning early in life, it will remain with them for the rest of their lives.
May your children be blessed with the love of learning, the love of their fellow mankind, and the love for their Maker.

PART I:

General Philosophy

MIND, BODY, AND SPIRIT ARE ONE.

"You have the potential to become anything to which you set your mind. You have a mind and a body and a spirit. With these three working together, you can walk the high road that leads to achievement and happiness. But this will require effort and sacrifice and faith.

You must get all of the education that you possibly can. Life has become so complex and competitive. You cannot assume that you have entitlements due you. "[1]

Gordon B. Hinckley, *Words of the Prophet: Seek Learning*

The mind, body, and spirit are directly connected to one another. I like to emphasize the three so that education doesn't become lopsided by trying to improve the mind

> *"To keep myself physically strong, mentally awake, and morally straight."*
>
> *Boy Scouts of America, Scout Oath*

only. Any change to one can or will affect the other. Your mind doesn't function well when your spirit is low or when your body comes down with the flu. Consider the Placebo Effect. A patient can be cured by taking pills made completely with sugar simply because the patient's mind thinks it a certain type of medication. A soldier's spirit to accomplish a mission could override the mind and body to do incredible things.

Physical activity for your child will help provide oxygen to the brain, build better stamina, and maintain focus. Studies have shown a correlation between Physical Education and grades.

Mark Levin sums up Antony Flew's, *THERE IS A GOD: How the world's most notorious atheist changed his mind.*

> "Reason and science can explain the existence of matter, but they cannot explain why there is matter. They can explain the existence of the universe, but they cannot explain why there is a universe. They can explain the existence of life, but they cannot explain why there is life. They can explain the existence of consciousness, but they cannot explain why there is consciousness." [2]

Spiritual development helps with the understanding of the *why*. Human understanding has its limits and is continually changing. Compare the science textbook and the bible from 200 years ago with the science textbook and bible of today. While the science textbooks have changed dramatically, the eternal truths of the bible have not. I believe that all truth comes from God, and someday science will catch up to the gospel.

> "The man of science is a poor philosopher."
> Albert Einstein

Dr. Henry Eyring, who received his Ph.D. from University of California Berkeley and served as president of the American Chemical Society, once said, "There are all kinds of contradictions in religion that I don't understand, but I find the same kinds of contradictions in science, and I haven't decided to apostatize from science."[3] Our priority for our children has been the spiritual development. Whenever there is a conflict of scheduling, church and church activities takes precedence over school 95% of the time.

From the words of Mr. Miyagi from the movie *Karate Kid*, "Keep balance Daniel-san." As you train and develop your child, keep the mind, body, and spirit working closely together.

GAME WITH A PURPOSE

Make it fun. Founder of Scouting, Lord Robert Baden-Powell said, "Scouting is a game with a purpose." I loved scouting as a youth. While earning my Eagle Scout rank, I didn't say I want to be a better leader or a better money manager or be a responsible citizen or learn how to set goals, ect. No. I wanted to go camping, fishing, hiking, exploring—I wanted to have fun.

Make learning fun. Learning can be a game with a purpose. A mark of a great learning program or activity is when the child does not know that he is learning. Fun makes the time go faster. Fun motivates the mind. Fun builds a desire for learning. In scouting, there are dishes to be washed and duties to be performed. In learning, there are tough books to be cracked and objectives to be performed. However, do your best to make it a game. Whenever considering any game, activity, or training, ask yourself if it will be fun for your child. Remember, learning can and should be fun.

NATURE VS. NURTURE

Genius is 1% inspiration and 99% perspiration

Thomas Edison

Is Nature at 1% and Nurture at 99% or is it 50/50? The debate on Nature vs. Nurture is ongoing. When it comes to Genius or the Child Prodigy, I lean more towards Thomas Edison's 99% perspiration. Arnold Schwarzenegger and other Mr. Universes or Mr. Olympians were not born with big biceps. Some are born more blessed than others when it comes to brain power. You could see in certain children that they are just naturals. Others (maybe many) like me are slow and struggle. However slow, I believe our minds are infinite and capable of great things. Excluding mental disability, the human mind can reach great heights.

Human mind refers to all humans (white, black, red, yellow, green, purple, and any shades under the rainbow). We are all spirit children of our Heavenly Father and were created in His image; therefore, our minds are infinite and capable of great things despite our racial genetic background. It is unfortunate that there are certain stereotypes for certain ethnic groups. If we apply Thomas Edison's 99% perspiration, then we could

> "Don't say burn baby burn; instead, learn baby learn, so you could earn baby earn."
>
> Dr. Martin Luther King, Jr.

assume that our genetic make-up accounts for the other 1%. I have recently read that 48% of "African-American" males graduate high school versus 76% of "White" males. Is this proof of genetic defect among the "African-American" population? Absolutely not. I believe that it is the outside environment of Gang Rap music and videos, the deterioration of fathers in the home, and other "influences" that plague the black community. Michelle Brown-Stafford, a parent of a 12 year-old college student and a 13 year-old high school freshman, wrote,

"People generally are astonished when I express my belief that my husband and I really haven't done anything miraculous in raising a child like Stephen. Perhaps it's because we are African-American, I'm not sure, for there were other mathematical prodigies of African origin long before our time. Then I notice Asian-American communities and how they are able to produce so many "Stephens". In fact they generate children deemed even more precocious at such astounding rates. I'm reasonably certain that the brain of our Asian brethren isn't any more complex than ours . . . aren't any bigger or made from any mutating DNA structure. My belief, however, is that their general attitude towards education and achievement is nurtured from birth—that it indeed becomes a lifestyle!"[4]

I agree wholeheartedly that the role of parents' attitudes towards education and achievement has a profound effect on the child. Michelle is an Accelerated Academic Strategist and her website is *www.mocha-charm.com*. For Chendara, Marcie, and Martha, being child prodigies has nothing to do with their being Asian or Mexican. Every questionnaire I get from a school or the census regarding my race, I put in "Human Race" on the "other" portion of the questionnaire. The only time race is important to me is when I do genealogy work to discover my ancestors. Throw out brain size, Darwin's theory, and skin color because we are all children of our Heavenly Father as the Declaration of Independence declares, " . . . all men are created equal . . ."

An undeniable Genius was Albert Einstein. He was dyslexic and didn't speak until the age of four. His I.Q. was not impressive. Yet, his passion and drive to discover the unknown was tremendous, even obsessive. At times he would hold a bell while he was studying, if he fell asleep while studying, the bell would fall to the ground and wake him up; then he would resume studying.

NO ONE CARES ABOUT YOUR CHILD
LIKE YOU DO—NO ONE!

Our children are our gems. They are precious and were entrusted to us by our Maker. We have a sacred responsibility to be the best stewards that we can for our children. There are good teachers, administrators, and caregivers out there. But none will be as good as you. The #1 advocates for our children is us. A popular radio talk personality Dr. Laura Schlessinger often says, "I am my kid's mom." Grandparents might come really close. However, no one—NO ONE cares more about our children like we, responsible parents, do.

Whenever a problem or a challenge arises, never raise the white flag until all of the options are exhausted. This is very true when it comes to the public school administration. Sometime the squeaky wheels get the grease. More times than not, I have found the answers and solutions when I am persistent enough.

Fight for your children. Do all you can that they may have the best possible education. The ultimate responsibility is yours, the parent. No amount of money put in the school system can replace the emphasis and encouragement on education that you provide within the walls of your home. Be in communication with their teachers. Request additional help from the school administration. No is not an option. If the school cannot help, look for other solutions.

PUBLIC SCHOOLS

When considering public schools, parents discover three facts—the good, the bad, and the ugly. As a child, I went through the Los Angeles Unified School System from K-12. All of our children have gone to public schools in three different states. For the most part, it has been a wonderful experience. I have learned to find the good, deal with the bad, and defeat the ugly.

THE GOOD: There are good teachers that work because they love the children. They are not just drawing a paycheck. Rather, they want to make the world a better place. For the most part, I think that they don't have tenure and have not been corrupted by the system. Some are good solid "old school" teachers who take their profession seriously all the way through their retirement. Some of these teachers spend money out of their pockets and spend extra time before and after school hours. They go to bat for our children, and we have to go to bat for them. Offer them help where they need it.

An English teacher in my 12th grade was great and helped changed my life. Other students thought that she was tough and mean. I thought of her as tough and caring. Our first day, she wanted us to write a page long essay before the class was over. At the end of class, I was nowhere near finished. She told me that if I wanted to pass the class I would have to put in a lot of effort. She offered to be available for students that wanted to come in during recess and lunch to do extra work. This wonderful teacher personally told me that I could do it. No one received an "A" grade. Only two students received a "B" grade in her class. I earned my "C". That was the best "C" grade that I have ever received in my entire life. I would put my 12th grade English teacher up against any in the top boarding schools in America.

THE BAD: My 7th grade science teacher once told me, "You will never amount to anything, Goofycorn." Goofycorn was another name for Jittakorn. He called me Goofycorn in private as well as in front of the entire class. As an adult working as an executive for the Boy Scouts, I had the opportunity to talk with a math class at a local high school. These students were 10th-12th grade students that were just barely learning percentage. Just before turning the time over to me, the teacher said to me in front of the entire class, "They will never amount to anything." I was shocked and angered. I didn't care what the teacher thought about what I planned to say because it became personal to me. I told the class about what my 7th grade teacher told me. Also, I told the students, "Never believe anyone that tells you that you will never amount to anything." I continued, "You could do anything, even be a great basketball player with the NBA." I asked how many NBA teams are there. How many players are on each team including the bench warmers? These children knew their basketball. We multiplied both numbers and got more than 600. I then asked how many people are in America. I didn't know the census numbers, but we made a big number. After the class and I worked the difficult division problem together, I explained to them that 0.01 is 1%. I asked them if our number was larger or smaller than 1%. Without hesitation, they all knew the answer. We went on and did some simple fraction to percentage conversion. I concluded that they could be anything they want. I also begged them to consider a back-up career plan and pursue education in case they don't achieve above top 1% or if they got injured. It was days like that make me wonder why I didn't become a teacher.

It is the bad teachers that shouldn't be near our children. Not only are they bad for the slow learning children, they are also bad for your child prodigy.

They believe that the poor students are hopeless and good students will be fine so why bother.

THE UGLY:

From time to time, we hear bad news about our public schools, for example, gang violence, teacher/student sexual relationships, free condoms, indoctrination of beliefs far different from our own, and sex education during kindergarten years. In addition, poorly performing teachers are not adequately addressed due to unions and job tenure. Poorly performing schools are not adequately addressed due to bureaucracies in the school system.

Mark Levin, a former top advisor and administrator to several members of President Reagan's cabinet, has some great ideas on improving the public schools. In his manifesto, he states that we should

> *Eliminate monopoly control of government education by applying the antitrust laws to the National Education Association and American Federation of Teachers; the monopoly is destructive of quality education and competition and is unresponsive to taxpayers who fund it.*

> *Eliminate tenure for government schoolteachers and college/university professors, making them accountable for the quality of instruction they provide students.*

> *Strip the statist agenda from curricula (such as multiculturalism and global warming) and replace it with curricula that reinforce actual education and the preservation of the civil society through its core principles.*

> *Eliminate the federal Department of Education, since education is primarily a state and local function.*[5]

For the most part, unions (local, state, and national) do more harm than good. This is because the primary question it asks is, "What is best for the teachers?" Rather than, "What is best for the children?" They could dress it up as, "We are here for the children." Those who are in charge of our kids should be asking themselves is, "Is this school good enough that I would put my own children in it?" I seriously doubt that our congressmen, senators, and top union bosses send their children to public schools.

The federal government needs to get out of our classrooms. Nowhere in the U.S. Constitution says that the federal government is responsible for educating our children. An example of this is the No Child Left Behind Act of 2001. Though well intended to make teachers more accountable, it has created problems. Those who want to better the system by doing whatever it takes to raise the scores of their standardized test, WILL NOT advance your child prodigy. Why would they want to advance your child when your child is doing great on the standardize tests? When teachers' bonuses and school funding is at stake, they are going to use your child prodigy to boost their scores. No way are they going to advance your child one, two, or more grade levels so that your child can only do "well" when they could do "great" just right where they are. We, child prodigy parents, need to call it No Child Advanced.

The nice thing about the No Child Left Behind is that we are able to look at individual schools' test results. Part of choosing a neighborhood to move into is based on the local scores of the school's standardize test results. Each State has its own website. The following three are the ones we have used.

California: *http://star.cde.ca.gov/star2006/Viewreport.asp*
Massachusetts: *http://www.doe.mass.edu/mcas/results.html*
Texas TAKS: *www.tea.state.tx.us/student.assessment/reporting/*

We use the results as a factor in selecting a school district. The scores are a good indicator, but I don't totally rely on the information. Chose the school before you chose the neighborhood. Do not pick your home and then go to any school that happens to be in your school's boundary. Use as much due diligence when shopping for a school as you would a home or a new car.

Locally, parents should have the right to chose where to send their children. School vouchers should be made available for public, private, or home school. Why should the parents who pay property tax that helps fund their local public school then have to fork out more money to send their children to private school, or spend their time and money to home school their own children? Parents will naturally shop for the best for their child. All of the schools (public, private, home) will have to compete if they want enrollments. If parents want to send their child across town to attend a better school, then let them. No local schools should have a monopoly based on boundaries.

Public education is a two way street. We have to do our part as parents. Bragg Elementary School in California, where our children attended, was a good example of what could happen when parents get involved. Parents were expected to do their fair share of grading homework, going on field trips, and participating in activities. The expectations came from other parents. We retained good teachers because they enjoyed our support. Likewise, the bad ones didn't last long because we had expectations for good teaching.

HOME SCHOOLS

Even though I have not home schooled in the literal sense, I have an admiration for all those that home school their children. Those who home school must have a determination and dedication because they use their time and money for the education of their own child.

The myth that homeschooled kids are not sociable is simply not true. The Home School Legal Defense Association commissioned a study to look at the "Homeschooling Grown Up." The finding showed that the adults that were homeschooled did very well concerning jobs, community activities, and voting. There are many social network groups for homeschoolers. Some of these networks are religious, interest, or location based. These network groups work together to go on field trips and participate in other activities.

Home Schooling students rank high on the national standardized test. According to the *Washington Times*[6] article, a study of almost 12,000 home-school students from all 50 states scored very high. The following are the results from five areas of academic pursuit:

- 84th percentile in Language.
- 84th percentile in Math.
- 86th percentile in Science.
- 84th percentile in Social Studies.
- 88th percentile in Core Studies (Reading, Language, and Math)

I'm sure that we could find one example of a homeschooler that does poorly, just as we could find one example of a public school student that does poorly; however, the average homeschooler's test results paints a clear picture that home school students ranks high.

DATE OF BIRTH DOES NOT DETERMINE
SOCIAL OR MATURITY LEVEL

Nothing makes my blood boil more than such statements as, "academically ready, but not socially ready" or "Not mature." These statements have been said to me on many occasions by the people of academia. DO NOT FALL FOR THIS PACK OF LIES. Yes, academic and social level are two different things. However, neither are necessarily bound by the other. The statement of "academically ready, but not socially ready" is repeated rapidly by many of the academia with little to no investigation of a child's situation. The truth of the matter is, they don't really care. It is as if somehow all the childhood maturity falls in line step based on age.

Assume that they are right and that all kids should be put in the same grade based on "age equals social/maturity level." Do we then abandon the consideration of academic levels? "A mind is a terrible thing to waste." A child still needs to be challenged and not be bored in class.

My hope is that K-12 will be more like colleges. One child's learning pace does not move at the same pace as the other children. Then why does K-12 move children along based on the age of the child? If I only took one class, I can't tell a university that I was a junior last year so they have to make me a senior this year. Likewise, the university is not going to say, "Sorry, you have to wait until your fourth year to graduate even though you took 21 units per semester and loaded up on summer courses." K-12, please do not move children along solely based on the age of the child.

Those who work with Special Needs children are themselves a special kind of people. I admire their love, patience, and dedication for the Special Needs children in need of great blessings. On the other side of the spectrum, children who are above average should also have their needs met.

Marcie (our 11 year-old) has many friends at Texas A&M—Texarkana. She is very active in many activities in the university. She is also a member of the Multi-Culture-Association and the Campus Activities Board at the college and faithfully attends their meetings and activities. Marcie is so popular with many students that Chendara is known as "Marcie's sister" and I am known as "Marcie's father."

The children do not need to be sheltered from children of different ages. Diversity in age and experience is good. Diversity in age reflects what goes on in colleges, the real world, and in the work place. I cannot say that I don't want to work with someone in the work place simply because I don't want to work with the "old" man.

If you can honestly evaluate your child, then you, and only you, know their social and maturity level. There is no such thing as a universal "maturity" or "social" evaluation and test that can be administered by the schools. So next time your are told, "academically ready but not socially ready," ask the school for a maturity/social testing.

TAKE TIME TO TEACH AND WORK

Before I move on, let's conduct an experiment.

1. Think of all of the great toys you have received as a child.

What did you think of? A bike? A video game? A doll? A train set? What happened to those toys? Are they properly displayed in your home for memories or ready to be passed on to your kids and grandkids or are they somewhere in a land field?

2. Now think of the great times your parent(s) spent with you.

If you are like me, you probably remember many of the great times that you and your parents have spent together. The times we went on a road trip to Yellow Stone Park will always be etched in my mind with great fond memories. The one and only time my dad helped me with Boy Scout fundraising was a day that I will never forget for the rest of my life.

Your list of time spent with your parents will be a lot longer than any toys that you have received on your birthday or Christmas. Now it is your turn to create great memories for your child. Why not share your time with them in educating them? Just 30 minutes a day reading to them or having them read could be a moment that they will remember for the rest of their lives. When you reflect upon these moments, you will realize that the time you spent will be no sacrifice at all.

LEFT BRAIN VS. RIGHT BRAIN

Neuroscientists theorize that each side of the brain controls two different modes of thinking.

Left Brain	Right Brain
• Objective	• Subjective
• Sequential	• Random
• Analytical	• Synthesizing
• Parts	• Wholes
• Rational	• Intuitive

This is perhaps why "opposites attract" with couples. One of the couple is an engineer and the other is an art painter. They both will complement each other and create synergism. Trekies (Star Trek fans) understand this very well. Dr. Spock (Left Brain) does many of the computations and analyzes the probabilities, then Captain Kirk (Right Brain) makes decisions based on the whole situation and intuitiveness.

Most of us tend to want to gravitate towards one side of the brain more than the other. This is natural because we become more accustom and familiar with one side over the other. For me, I was more into math (Left Brain). Since my reading, writing, and articulating skills were poor during my early childhood, I turned to math for refuge. In my math world (non subjective), no one could judge me. I was either right or wrong. Even my math teachers could not dispute my methods as long as I came up with the right answer. Unfortunately to this day, when I see an abstract sculpture outside of a building, I don't get it. If teachers gave credit for day dreaming (Right Brain) in class, then I would have graduated early from high school. Today, I find it a pleasure to venture in the Right Realm. I enjoy going to plays and listening to orchestras. I am a big admirer of Norman Rockwell's and Thomas Kinkade's art work.

Your child prodigy should be able to navigate comfortably back and forth from left to right side of the brain. This is not only good for the child's collective well roundedness, but also for the first two years of college. The General Education is the lower division portion of the degree plan for the four year college. See **Appendix A** *http://www.cccua.edu/public/userfiles/files/ Degree%20Plans/AA/AA-Fast%20Track.pdf* of the Cossatot Community College AA Fast Track Degree Plan. The General education is designed to help a student be better well rounded. From Math to Fine Arts, from Natural Science to Social Science, and from History to Government, the first two years are designed to help a student develop the whole brain. Develop a learning program for your child that includes both sides of the brain.

From the words of Mr. Miyagi from the movie Karate Kid, "Keep balance, Daniel-san." As you train and develop your child, mix and match games and activities that are both Left & Right Brained.

BRAIN BUILDING IS LIKE BODY BUILDING

Training the brain is very much like training the body. The brain needs light study at times. Other times, it needs heavy and intense studying. In any good athletic training program, there is ALWAYS scheduling for rest. If you want to find a good educational technique or program, just get advice from any athletic coach or body work out book. Then substitute the entire words "workout" with the word "study" from the coach or book. For example:

- 30 minutes of upper body 3 times this week is translated to 30minutes of studying subject #1 for 3 times this week.
- 30 minutes of lower body 3 times this week is translated to 30minutes of studying subject #2 for 3 times this week.

- 20 minutes of cardio everyday this week is translated to 20 minutes of studying subject #3 everyday this week.
- Heavy workout this Saturday is translated to heavy studying, or test, this Saturday.
- .... and so on.
- Rest this Sunday is translated to Rest this Sunday.

I finished the Los Angeles Marathon in 2004.[7] For my training for the marathon, I used a book by Jeff Galloway called _Galloway's Book on Running_.[8] I enjoyed long distance running because it gave me thinking time. While jogging one time, IT HIT ME! Training for the run to accomplish the marathon is just like learning techniques I used while taking classes to graduate college! This discovery leads me to believe three major principles; 1. Repetition 2. Transition. 3. Progression. While training in the gym, I often work out on cardio. From time to time, I do go to the free weight section. In the free weight area, I also observe the "repetition, transition, and progression" principles being applied. The body builders would either have a buddy (spotters) or a personal trainer. I would like to use the subject of math to help illustrate because I feel that it applies directly to this principle.

1.   Repetition. Some body builders have cards to tell them how many reps (number of times) they have to do. Each rep also has a number of sets. For example, 20 reps would be how many bench presses they would do. If they have a "set" of 3, they would do 20 bench press, rest, then 20 more, rest, then the final 20, thus making it 3 sets of 20 reps. There could be a multiple number of sets and various types of sets done in the course of one work out.

Repetition may not be one of the most fun or romantic parts of training. However, it is vital. Repetition helps gain proficiency and builds endurance. When I first ran a mile, it was hard. After running a mile, day after day, it became much easier. When it became easier, I wanted to run farther. When using math flash cards of simple additions over and over again with your child, it will eventually get much easier, so much easier that your child will want to move on. Equations need to be worked on over and over again. Even though you know and understand an equation, you still need to practice it repeatedly.

2. Transition: Going To the Next Level. Once the repetition has gone its course, then you need to push the envelope to take it to the next level. In weight lifting, this is where one has to try to go as far as he or she can. This is why a spotter is important because if one could only bench halfway, the weights will fall down on him. This is the fine line between reaching the maximum potential and muscle failure.

Spotters are the ones responsible for the safety of the weight lifter. In the gym weight room, I often see a body builder's spotter pushing, yelling, and sometime cursing at the body builder to give encouragement to go further. Do not yell or curse at your kid. Yelling and cursing is a guy to guy way of saying, "I love you man, and I believe in you." When transitioning your child from the normal repetitious studying to a new concept with any subject, give your child plenty of encouragement.

Muscles will grow and develop while resting after a hard work out session. Likewise, the mind will grow and develop while resting after a hard learning session. Consider the following illustrations of neurological growth in the brain:

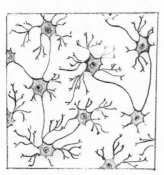

Neurons Before Learning

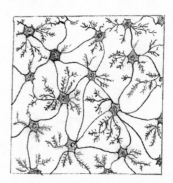

Neurons After Learning

Neurons before Learning   Neurons after Learning

Continuously reaching maximum weight and muscle failure will only cause burn-out and muscle break-down. Even the toughest drill sergeant at a military boot camp will not prescribe a 24-7 intense physical training. The transition period is only a short time used to get to the next level.

3. Progression. Progression now becomes repetition. Once the lower level of the subject is mastered, then the child is ready to move on.

Looking at it from running prospective: One mile per day for 14 days (repetition), 2 miles per day for 2 days (Transition), and then 1 ¼ mile per day for 14 days (progression).

In Isaiah 28:10 we read, "For precept must be upon precept, precept upon precept; line upon line, line upon line; here a little, and there a little:" Also, biceps upon biceps, and miles upon miles. The goal of a marathon runner is to go faster for the 26.2 miles. The goal of a body builder is to gain more body mass. The goal of your prodigy child is to be academically prepared (knowledge upon knowledge) for college entrance.

Resting. While physically resting, the body rebuilds and grows. While mentally resting, your mind also rebuilds and grows. Have you ever been stuck with something you are trying to think about or solve and just can't get it? Then you walk away and not think about it anymore. Then out of nowhere, the idea comes to you. NOT resting and cramming will NOT help improve your child's education. Rather, your child will be turned-off from learning.

Remember, brain training is like body training. The mind, body, and spirit are one. Physical training is structured. The learning process is the same way. Yet, too many people go randomly back and forth, grabbing information here and grabbing information there. Have a structured program that follows the body building principles.

Keeping a good balance of reward is hard and tricky. Like the Maslow's Hierarchy of Needs, Jet's Learning Reward System also has a hierarchy. At the bottom is the bribe "Learn to Get," then "Positive Reinforcement," finally, at the top is "Pay to Learn."

Many experts warn against excessive reward (bribing) for good reasons. Children may constantly look for reward in order for them to learn. Bribing could put reward at odds with learning. In other words, the child may ask him/herself, "Do I want the bribe to learn or could I go without the bribe so I don't have to learn." Learning should be a reward in itself. Bribing is a short term fix. When a child learns for reward, who will be there to bribe the child when he or she becomes an adult? Giving out rewards is good from time to time as a quick motivator. However, beware of the dangers of excessive bribes.

Having warned of the dangers of bribing, we love to reward our children. Bribes come before learning, "I will give you X, if you will study." Positive reinforcements come after learning and are usually random without any promises. Positive reinforcement is the key. Reward does not necessary mean a toy, food, or monetary goods, although it can be. Words of sincere praise like "You're doing a fine job," or "That is awesome," or "We are proud of you." We see the joy in our children's faces when we praise them. A pat on the back or a high five also lifts up the spirit. The reward for finishing a book is going shopping for another book to read. Positive reinforcements should be immediate.

Chendara was the only child that we used vegetables as a form of positive reinforcement. We would say, "Wow Chendara! That was good, now you get a carrot." Today, Chendara is the only one of five children that wants to eat vegetables.

The Boy Scouts of America has an affective reward system. Merit badges, rank advancements, and patches are very enticing. As a young Scout in the 80's, my scoutmaster would conduct "mini-court-of-honors" so that he could reward us with "skill awards" belt loops that would go on our belts. These instant gratifications kept me going.

We often stress to our children that education is not free. Education is of a great value and it has a price tag on it. Books and materials cost money, and people's time has value attached to it. Learning is something that will last them a life time. While Chendara was attending Cossatot Community College, she worked at our convenient store to help pay for her tuition and textbooks. Marcie also helps at the store for her education. When the girls shop for textbooks, they look for used books at the campus bookstore or go online to save money.

Learning should be fun that is a reward within itself. However, praises and goodies are appreciated. We let our children know that good grades are their rewards. A good education and a college degree will be their rewards in the future.

WE SEEK AFTER THESE THINGS

In the Book of Philippians and in the *Thirteenth Article of Faith,* we read, "If there is anything *virtuous, lovely,* or of good report or praiseworthy, we seek after these things." We have tried just about everything that was of "good report." Things that we have read about, advised by other parents, recommended by teachers and others, we have tried just about all of them. Thank goodness there were no books stating the exact thing we had to do. Since we had lots of trial and error, it allowed us to modify and fit different learning games to different children.

Many products on the market are well intended. I have ordered both Hooked on Phonics & My Baby Can Read during late night infomercials. Many online retailers such as Amazon and Ebay have ratings from consumers. On my iPad, I look for the stars where other people have rated and consult reviews from other parents before I purchase an App. I hope someday there will be a website for parents like yourselves to write your reviews as you raise your child prodigy.

PART II:

Programs, Activities, and Games

It was a very early morning the day after Thanksgiving (Black Friday). We decided to go to one of our favorite learning/discovery stores in the local major mall because they had a sale on an educational game we wanted. While walking to our store, we passed by a major toy chain store. The long line was stretched out to an amazing distance. Shopping was an ease at our learning store and there was little to no line. While comparing the two stores, I was left with no doubt in my mind where the parents put their priorities. When we hear of poor performance in the school systems, the parents must take some of the blame.

We supplement our kids with programs, activities, and games that go beyond public school. We enjoy investing our money and time with our children. Just 10 to 30 minutes per day does wonders. When the kids get home, the first priority is homework from school. My wife and I would take turns helping with the homework. After homework, my wife and I would take turns playing different learning related games and activities with our children. We mainly work on the 3 R's (reading, writing, and arithmetic). However, sometimes we would try to cover other subjects. Mondays was family outing or spiritual learning day. Monday's activity was movie night or mini road trips to somewhere local. Tuesdays through Fridays, we use various learning activities. Saturdays was kind of a hodgepodge. Sunday was a day of rest.

Depending on your work schedule and your children needs, you will want to design your own learning activity times with your child. I wish you the best adventures as you train your prodigy child that goes beyond what they receive at school.

Again, the following list of programs, activities, and games are just some of the things we have done. I hope some of it works for you. I hope you will find some that are even better than the ones we have found. Always remember the FUN.

MUSIC: BEFORE BIRTH AND BEYOND

Training of prodigy begins in the womb. We have heard the Mozart Effect. The theory states that listening to Mozart's music helps improve the I.Q. We play classical music to our children while they are still in the womb. Can the unborn hear music? Does Mozart or other classical music help improve the mental state? Are we fanatical parents with too much time on our hands? I don't really know the answer to any of the questions. The volume of the music was at a low enough decibels that it couldn't have done any damage to the children's ear drums. Today, none of our children has reported any hearing trouble. When we look at the live ultrasound, we know that there is a live human being in the womb. I also know that those times playing music to our unborn were also good private time for my wife and me. It also helps put us in a mind-set that we are fully committed in our children's education.

We also sing the alphabet song to our children while they are in the womb. We continue to sing it to them until they are able to recognize each letter of the alphabet. The sound of our voices and the rhythm to the song brings comfort to a child. By singing it 2-4 times per day, the child develops a familiarity with the alphabet.

We still believe in the Mozart Effect. From time to time, we play classical music around the house and before the kids go to bed. Music has quite an effect on our thinking and mood. It can influence our thinking for the good or the bad. Older music can bring us back to a certain time and certain location. Pink Floyd's *"Another Brick In The Wall"* was and is one of my all time favorites. I watch it on You Tube from time to time because it brings me back to the age of innocence. However, with lyrics like, "We don't need no education . . ." or "Hey, teachers, leave those kids alone." Inspired me not to do my homework and viewed my teachers as an adversary rather than an advocate. Consider good wholesome music for your child. Consider the compositions of Mozart, Chopin, Beethoven, Bach, and other classical artists as smart music for the brain.

BABY EINSTEIN VIDEO

BABY EINSTEIN™ DVDs are heaven sent. Ratings from Amazon.com customers is close to 5/5. Our kids could watch and re-watch these DVDs many times when they were little. The video plays classical music while the screen entertains with various objects and movements. If there is such a thing as "too much of a good thing," BABY EINSTEIN™ is not.

This is a good ploy when you need a little break. We use them when we are preparing meals, morning, day, and night time before bed. They now have a large variety of favorite DVDs that we can swap out.

HOOKED ON PHONICS

The one we used from this company was the mid-late 1990's version. This version was absolutely wonderful. It also helped my wife and me with our reading skills. The entire program took the child from learning the alphabet to reading words and to complete sentences. The vital part of these activities was that it was structured and had rules. The structure is a neat step-by-step approach that for once in my life I understand. The exceptions to the rules are not too many in number. For me, it was easier to comprehend by sounding out each letter than to memorize each word by word as in sight words. The methods and steps are

1. Learn the letters of the alphabet
2. Learn the sound of each letter of the alphabet
3. Combine three letters to make simple three letter words.

Another valued program by Hooked on Phonics is the Hooked on Phonics Master Reader™. This program helps children become more efficient readers. There are 40 levels in the game. Each has a computer session and a physical reading assignment. For every 10th level, there is a book to read. The computer sessions run like this:

- Chop It!—this is one of the many games on master reader. This helps your child chop a word into syllables. This teaches your child how to separate a word into syllables. This also makes reading easier, because the child reads the word in chunks.
- Build It!—this tests your child's word making skills. It makes your child make as many real words as they can with the first and last couple of words. If your child misses some words then the computer will make the words. Build it (2) is the same thing except this one lets your child build bigger words.

- Whack It!—a word clue is stated verbally by the narrator. As the words appear on the screen, you need to click on the word that matches the word stated by the narrator.
- See It, Say It!—when a word appears on the screen, you say the word. Afterward, the game will say the word to help reinforce that the child says it properly.

The reading assignment on each level reinforces what the child has played on the computer. This is a must-have game that will entertain and improve your child's reading skills. Once your child has some basics in reading, I highly recommend this game.

SIGHT WORDS

Although the phonics method, to me, is the better method than sight words; we still want to utilize as many methods as possible. Sight words reinforce reading. Most common words that a child will encounter are used. Some of the phonics rules do not apply to the sight words. By learning and memorizing the sight words, the reader's speed and confidence will increase.

My wife would print out sight words and post them all over the house. They would go in the kid's rooms, living room, kitchen, bathroom, dining room, hall ways, all over. She would post one word at a time. The word would stay up for 1-5 days depending on the word. From time to time during the day, we would quiz them.

FLASH CARDS

We used flash cards when the children were as young as 1 years-old all the way to about 5th grade. It works so well because it is both repetitive and progressive. We use flash cards with pictures for the first stage. Everyday objects and animal pictures seem to be popular with our children. We find it useful for sight words and math. In college, our daughters use index cards to make their own flash cards for memorization. The Apple® Ipad app has flash cards from ABC to GRE (testing for college Graduate Entrance and Admission).

Start with 2-5 cards. Once the child masters them and feels good and confident, then add one or two more to the deck. This way, the child will learn new ones while identifying the previous cards. Continue to add one or two more to the deck. After a while, start removing the original cards or

www.raisingchildprodigy.com

the ones that the child has totally mastered. If you continue to use the older cards, you could insult their intelligence and they will become bored.

Make a game of it. The ones they get right, they get to keep. "WOW! You sure got a lot of cards" The ones they don't get right put on a separate pile. Use it as an "it's okay to fail" teachable moment and work with them just on the wrong pile. Go over each of the wrong ones and work with them. As they get each right, reshuffle the card back with the right pile.

Flash cards are a big confidence builder. We could see the joy in their eyes as they were able to take on more and more cards.

YOUR BABY CAN READ!®

I thought I would try this program when the twins were five years old. Jared has a hard time reading and I thought he could use some extra help. The program looks very good and promising. However, the boys didn't like it because they said, "it is for babies." Had the title been called, "My Big Boys Can Read" and used older kids in the video, they would have liked it. After trying to sell the twins to use the program for a day and a half, they didn't buy it.

Not letting a good program go to waste, I let a friend at church with a baby use the first video. She said her baby loved it. After two months, she wanted to get the 2nd video. It worked so great that I let her use the entire program. I told her that she could use it until our first grandchild is born.

Your Baby Can Read!® is basically flash cards on video. One advice I would give to Your Baby Can Read!® would be to develop Big Kids Can Read! This could also be a big hit. Just use more advance words with older kids on the video.

PIANO LESSONS

Piano is a good gateway to other instruments. You learn to read music sheets and use your motor skill. If your child wants to go into any other instrument, they could easily transition from piano. I believe that learning music notes is like learning another language. In fact, music (along with math) is truly a universal language. When I was at the World Scout Jamboree in Thailand and the World Scout Jamboree in England, I enjoyed watching young scouts from different parts of the world with different musical instrument play together. It was a wonderful site to see, a true world unity. Many experts believe that those who are multilingual are better learners.

According an article written by Jennifer W. Miner on the *www. musicappreciation.suite101.com* website, benefits of piano lessons for children are

- **Increased hand-eye coordination**. Helps with writing skills.
- **Improved concentration.** Learning piano takes focus. Reading music requires translating the written notes into music with the correct tempo and rhythm.
- **Improved school performance.** A study by Francis Rauscher in 2000 revealed that playing piano helped kids understand concepts behind science, math, and even engineering.
- **Music appreciation.** By understanding the process of individual notes that make up a whole musical composition, engages children in a deeper understanding of the complexity of music. This carries through to a lifetime of music appreciation, across musical genres.
- **Being well-rounded.** Most children don't end up as concert pianists. However, having piano as a hobby helps if a child also has other hobbies and interests.
- **Confidence.** The self-esteem boost that comes from mastering any musical instrument is considerable.

What age to start? Chendara started at 9 years old, Marcie started at 7 years old, Robert started at 7, and Jacob and Jared started at 5 years old. Again, each child is different. For us, it was a matter of the music instructors' availability and our personal situation at the time.

Each of our children benefited from recitals. We had good instructors that had the children play in front of audiences. Whether it was in front of family, other students, or in competition, the kids gained confidences by performing live.

Chendara and Marcie use their piano skills to bless the elderly. They played in rest homes to the enjoyment of wrinkly, smiley faces.

Chendara uses piano to relief stress. While on the fast track at Cossatot Community College, she would practice and play her piano before exams and finals. She was in her own little world before she studied or wrote a term paper. She could be on the piano for minutes to hours. When she was finished, I could see the stress disappear.

ROAD TRIPS

Our family loves road trips. Sometimes we go to the local park and other times we will go across states. The kids enjoy long trips that involve motels and restaurants because they don't have to clean up after themselves. It is a good time to spend together while experiencing what this great country has to offer. We make stops at just about any place that seems interesting. The journey can be as fun as the destination.

> *"On the road again . .Goin' places that I've never been. Seein' things that I may never see again. I can't wait to get on the road again . ."*
>
> *Willie Nelson*

Your child could only get so much out of reading books. Get out there into the real world. Especially if they have read about something, then actually going to see it. Reading alone can't do justice to our sense of smell, taste, touch, sound, and sight (3D) unless we are really there. Going to places helps reinforce what we have read.

When you have children in the car that is moving 70 miles per hour, you automatically have a captive audience. We sang songs and play rhyme games, "I spy," or alpha finder. I can't seem to get "Old McDonald" out of my head from our recent road trip. In "Old McDonald," you are not allowed to repeat any animal that has already been used, otherwise you would be eliminated. The song continues until there is only one person left. In our rhyme game, one person would say a word, then anybody could continue to say another word that rhymes until there is no more word that rhyme. In our alpha finder game, we look for letters from anything we see on the road. We start from the letter A and work ourselves all the way to the letter Z. We also test simple math. We try to do our best to stimulate the mind while on the road.

MUSEUM, ZOO, AND AQUARIUM

Museums, zoos, and aquariums are theme parks for the mind. When we lived in Long Beach, California, we had family memberships to the Los Angeles Zoo and the Aquarium of The Pacific, Long Beach. The Aquarium annual membership pass is $110 for the entire family for the entire year. What a bargain! I believe that the L.A. Zoo was about the same price. The children never tired of looking at animals. There is something about nature and animals that draws us to it. To keep the cost down, we also pack our own lunch and use the provided picnic tables. These are very low cost and high stimulus activities. These outings makes it easier to learn and talk about the food chain, eco systems, water cycles, habitat, environment, and much more. While animals are mating, this is also an opportunity to conduct sex education.

Museums of science, art, history, and others are also great ways for a family to have an outing. It opens young minds to new things and reinforces some of the things that they have learned in books and schools. While at "theme parks for the mind," the child also sees and interact with other children.

LEGO®

My best friend, Jared L. Low, and I played with wooden blocks growing up. We would spend hours building all sorts of things. We would build a city and drive our little Hot Wheels around it. When we were finished, we would have fun tearing it down. Then we would either build something else or put them away and go and play some other things. When Jared's dad finished with a construction project, we would get the scraps and sand them down and add them to our set of blocks. Looking back, I can't believe we had so much fun with wood. In addition to fun, I believe that our play helped build both our left and right side of the brain. We had to think logically on the soundness of our structure and be creative to insure its coolness. Today, Jared is a computer engineer in Austin, Texas.

Lego is a big hit with Marcie and all of our boys and has served the same purpose as it did for Jared and me when we were kids playing with blocks. Today's Lego is amazing. There are so many varieties of sets, shapes, and colors. When you get a set, make sure to encourage your child to build it like the picture by following the instruction. This not only helps them with logically following the instructions, but it might be the only time they will have all of the pieces before they start losing them. I am amazed by the things the boys build out of Lego's. They could spend hours building and rebuilding. Marcie likes to build complex Lego sets and display them in her room. Lego is a true game with a purpose.

COMPUTER & TECHNOLOGY

Technology is here to stay. Kids today will need to learn to type, use various software, and be comfortable with the internet at a very young age. More and more college courses are online. Computer is an important tool for school, personal, and work. The key word is "tool." It is NOT a babysitter and it CANNOT be your kid's teacher. Technology is a great tool when used appropriately.

There is much wonderful software that is educational as well as fun. Some is purely educational and some is pure fun which we use as part of a reward system. Since there are so many computer games in the market, I suggest looking at the ratings and reading the reviews. When in doubt, buy it! There is one that we absolutely love and highly recommend. All five of our kids have played with Elmo's Preschool. Elmo's Preschool has letters, numbers, shapes, and music. It is solid software for getting kids ready for kindergarten. Come on, how could you not like Elmo? He is too cute.

Preschool games allow your children to get used to the mouse. Eventually, they will need to learn to type unless someone comes up with a flawless voice recognition to key in the words. About five is a good age to start to learn to type. Jumpstart Typing by Knowledge Adventure can do the trick. It has a pre test and then sets your goals based on your test. As you pick up your speed and do well at different games, you slowly unlock the professor until he is completely freed. When you monitor your child, stress that speed is not the most important thing. Stress that finger placement and not looking at the keyboard is important. I made the mistake of turning on the computer and letting Marcie go at it. She went at it alright. She was super fast. Later, I notice she was taking a long time typing up one of her short essays. Trying to retrain her how to type was harder because I had to monitor her typing form.

I have heard that internet filters are good. We make sure that the computers are not privately located in the house. Internet has lots of good as well as bad. Our enemies are only a click away. Images of pornography could cause a long term or even permanent damage to these young minds and spirits. When used properly, the internet is a wealth of information and recourses.

LEAP FROG®, LEAPSTER®, TAG™

The Leap Frog (LF) line of products uses amazing technology. The researchers and developers at LF deserve some major awards. In addition to my kids, I have seen many children use (play & learn) these products hours at a time. Lord Baden Powell would have been proud of how LF lived up to the phrase, "game with a purpose." These make great gifts for your children, nieces, and nephews. Next time you see them on the isles of major a department store, put one in your shopping cart and you will quickly see what I mean.

The LF Tag book looks like a normal book. However, the magic is in the pen. When kids move the pen along the word, the pen sounds out the word. Kids could go back to the word(s) as many times as they like until they are comfortable with the word(s). The pen will also sound out the word of the picture that a child points to. For the most part, the kids know what the pictures are, but it is still fun to point.

The LF Leapster is wonderful alternative to the traditional hand held games such as Nintendo. Amazon.com Hands-On Review states,

> The Leapster Explorer Learning Game System from LeapFrog is an exciting, handheld gaming device that includes preset games and videos, and boasts plenty of downloadable features and cartridges. This durable handheld device for kids aged 4 to 9 years plays Leapster Explorer e-books, games, videos, and more. With the Leapster Explorer, kids practice a range of skills—from reading and writing to math and sciences—through play and entertainment.

COLLEGE PREPARATION BOOKS AND MATERIALS

It is challenging to find text books, workbooks, and activity books that will help them prepare for college. The main resource that we use is the community colleges book store. The developmental courses that are offered at the community colleges help prepare students to take "college level" courses. These college level courses are Freshman Composition and College Algebra. Also, the developmental reading class helps prepare students to read at a college level. These developmental course credits do not apply to the degree. Rather, they are prerequisites for taking college level courses. The clerk at the front desk can assist with knowing which books and materials are needed for the correct course. Start with the lowest level course first and go from there as needed.

Local high schools will be another good place to look into. Once you find out what textbooks they are using and fits your child, you could shop online using the ISBN number. Local big box bookstores could be useful if you know what you are looking for. Many of the Parent/Teacher stores are very knowledgeable with what you need for high school curriculum and college prep. The books and materials used should compliment with preparing and improving for college entrance exam test.

READING

I put this as a last item because it is the most important. Reading needs to be the first focus for a child. When it comes to learning, there is no debate or argument that reading is the MOST IMPORTANT. No child could succeed in college

> *"the last shall be first, and the first last"*
>
> *Matthew 20:16*

without being a proficient reader. Reading is the gateway to knowledge, adventure, imagination, and even wisdom. Books should be viewed as a reward. The path to good reading and learning is fun.

Read to your newborn. This is a good time for you to practice your story telling talents. Practice your narrative, tone, volume, sound effects, pauses, and speed to bring the book alive. It is safe to say that a brand new month-old baby will not have any vocabulary comprehension. However, reading to a child at the earliest age creates structure and familiarity. In addition, your children will hear the sweet sound of your voice. Eventually they will see a pattern of reading by you turning the pages and pointing to pictures. There are plenty of baby books on the market. The ones with animals seem to be popular with our kids. Even at infancy, you could never go wrong with Dr. Seuss books.

> *"A capacity and taste for reading gives access to whatever has already been discovered by others."*
>
> *Abraham Lincoln*

Casual reading is merely sounding out the words without any comprehension. Active reading is decoding the meaning from the book and the author. While reading, engage your child with some stimulating questions.

PART III:

College Admissions & Preparations

College admissions vary as much as colleges. I have had good experiences with all of them except one. Most institutions want to increase their enrollment for qualifying students. The Colleges that I have dealt with and at least one of my children has attended are:

1. Cossatot Community College. DeQueen, Arkansas.
    I LOVE this college. From the administration, to the instructors, to the support staff, everyone has been very friendly and helpful. They have campuses in DeQueen, Ashdown, and Nashville. Chendara graduated with an

    > *"Learn More, Live Better."*
    >
    > *Cossatot Community College*
    > *University of Arkansas*

    Associates Degree at age 15. Marcie took 5 classes that tremendously prepared her to be admitted to Texas A&M—Texarkana at age 10.

2. Texas A&M University—Texarkana. Texarkana, Texas.
    Admissions have been very professional. There is no age discrimination whatsoever. The answers that they didn't know, they did their best to find out. A&M-Texarkana gave Chendara full admissions at age 14. A&M-Texarkana had their first Freshman Class in the fall of 2010.

Marcie was part of the first Freshman Class with full admissions at age 10. Since Marcie was so young, they assigned her a personal

> *"Our goal is to produce quality graduates within a career-oriented curriculum."*
>
> *Dr. C.B. Rathburn, III-President A&M-Texarkana*

advisor so that she could go for help anytime.

3. Cerritos Community College. Norwalk, California
   I am a little biased because I am an alumnus. Cerritos is one of the

> *"Driven by the pursuit of unparalleled student success, Cerritos College will provide access to innovative learning opportunities that promote the power of learning."*
>
> *Cerritos Community College's Vision*

top rated community colleges in Southern California. Chendara was 8 when she took her first college class. The dean of admissions was very welcoming and only required a written permission from the principal of the elementary school. Chendara did very well and has an official transcript. The dean of admissions wanted Chendara to beat the school's graduate record of 12 years old. We didn't pursue any more college at the time because Bragg Elementary School's GATE (gifted and talented education) was a good challenge for Chendara and we were afraid of her missing out on her childhood. A++ for Cerritos Community College.

4. Brigham Young University (BYU). Provo, Utah
   We took the opportunity of the Visiting Student Program. This gave Chendara a chance to live in a dorm and experience the big campus life. Students from

> *"To assist individuals in their quest for perfection and eternal life."*
>
> *The Mission Statement of BYU*

other universities could take classes in their Spring and Summer sessions. Admissions was very internet driven. BYU is owned and operated by the Church of Jesus Christ of Latter-Day-Saints. You do not have to be a member to be admitted. It is ranked 4th for the most strict college. A strict Code of Conduct is what we like to hear for our teenage daughter to spend the summer away from home.

5. Southern Arkansas University (SAU). Magnolia, Arkansas
This is an amazing university. The staff constantly goes out of their way to make sure you get the WOW effect. If you ask a question that they don't have the answer to, they will go to great lengths to find it for you. When you ask for directions, they will physically take you

> *"A Tradition of Success for 100 Years."*
>
> *Sothern Arkansas University*

to your destination. Marcie took Trigonometry with Professor Sutherland. He allowed me to sit in so that I could relearn Trig. His instructions and explanations were phenomenal. SAU = WOW.

6. Texarkana College. Texarkana, Texas
Not child prodigy friendly for me. Please read **Appendix B** from the *Inside Higher Ed*, *"Age bias case: Is 13 too young for community college?"* The current president, James H. Russell, has been on the job for a week (June 2011). He apologized for the past and hopes that things will be better in the future.

Some of the factors of college admissions include but are not limited to:

- ACT or SAT scores
- GPA
- Admission policy
- Personality and attitude of the Dean/Director of Admissions.

The admissions requirements and procedure are in all of the colleges' catalogs. You may also find them on the school's websites. Work close with the gate keeper (head of admissions). They try to be very fair. They not only are trying to accommodate your needs, but also have to look out for the best interest of their institution.

AUDITING (NO CREDIT) COLLEGE CLASSES

I highly recommend your child "audit" a class before trying to gain full admissions. There are many benefits for auditing. Auditing is like a free trail. It allows you to see how well your child adapts to a classroom full of adults, to see if your child could follow the syllabus and keep up assignments without the teacher pinning a note on your child's t-shirt, and to see if your child could benefit and thrive in a college environment. This is also a free trial period for the school as well. The college administration has an opportunity to evaluate your child. This is a win-win for both parties.

Technically, when auditing, you are only an observer. You may take notes and learn. At Cerritos Community College, auditing allows your child to take a college course without the commitment to receive a grade but receive full credit (pass/no pass). Many (if not all) community colleges offer courses that are developmental and prerequisites for Freshman Composition, or College Algebra. They also offer reading courses that help the students obtain the college reading level.

> *"Live as if you were to die tomorrow. Learn as if you were to live forever."*
>
> Gandhi

Taking our children to their first day of college was tougher than taking them to their first day of kindergarten. With a prodigy child, it really isn't that long ago. Unlike being with kids their own age in kindergarten, now they will be in class with adults. We have impressed a couple of things to our children before they take their first step into a college class:

- Ecclesiastes chapter 3, "To everything there is a season, and a time to every purpose under the heaven." A great complimentary song to this scripture is by The Byrds called *Turn! Turn! Turn!* There is a time to play, a time to laugh, a time to work, a time to learn. Their time in college class is to do their best to behave as an adult. When in Rome, do as the Romans; when with adults, do as the adults.

- You can do the work. Your test has proved that they deserve to be in the class. Do not be intimidated.

Marcie was on the President's List for having straight "A"s as a full time student. Chendara graduated Magna Cum Laude and has a recommendation for Honor's Scholarship to Texas A&M (**See Appendix C**) from CCCUA.

- HAVE FUN! Enjoy yourself and have fun.

COLLEGE ENTRANCE EXAM

The ACT and the SAT are the two exams that the colleges use as part of their entrance requirement. Preference on the ACT or SAT will depend on the region and the schools' entrance requirement. Some might require both. The colleges around our area require the ACT. There are different publishers that have the ACT preparation. In the textbook, you will find strategies and some tests. The tests are very similar to the actual tests.

Take it early and take it often. The more your child takes the test, the more he will be conditioned to it. Also, he will eventually spend no time reading the instructions and all the precious time on the actual test. The obvious reason for these tests is to measure the knowledge of the subject. Not so obvious is that it is designed to stress the test taker. The time allotted on each section is designed so that the test taker cannot finish every question. By taking it early and often, it exposes your child to stress

> *"It's not that I'm so smart, it's just that I stay with problems longer."*
>
> *Albert Einstein*

and pressure. The similar stress and pressure will be the same ones your child will face in college. Projects, exams, midterms, and the gauntlet of final exams are part of the college life.

There are some things to know about taking the ACT test for the first time. Once a child is doing 8th-9th grade level work, then it is a good time to take the test. Although the materials cover up to the 12th grade, your child should still take it for the conditioning and the exposure to stress and pressure. Let your child know that it is not for score. It is only for him to be comfortable with the test. As you administer the test from the ACT preparation book, stay strictly to the time and make it as real as possible. Give

> *"That which we persist in doing becomes easier for us to do; not that the nature of the thing is changed, but that our power to do is increased."*
>
> *Heber J. Grant*

you child something to look forward to after the test. Maybe going to the movie or out to dinner. Again, let your child know that it is not for a score, only for him to be comfortable with the test. After the first test, shortly review some strengths and weaknesses. Then, go out and have lots of fun.

Take the practice test from the preparation book about once a month or every other month. Improving the scores would be nice, but that is not the reason for taking the test. Remember, conditioning is the purpose. By evaluating the results, you may want to use it to tailor your kid's subjects or materials.

When your child is comfortable and familiar with the test, register him or her to take the real ACT test. Let your child get a chance to feel the real deal. Also, it will take out the mystery of the ACT TEST that is out there somewhere. Go to www.actstudent.org and register. The fee is $32 (No Writing). Compared to potential dollars in scholarships and entrance to a college, $32 is a sound investment. Never "Send your scores" to any institution. Even if your child is hot and 100% sure of the college of choice, never "Send your scores" to any institution when registering for a test. Your child may have one bad day and flop on the test. At minimum, it will take the pressure of your child into thinking "this is it." They can take the test as many times as they like, and their ACT account will keep all the scores for them. Once you get the score back and are satisfied with it, then you can instruct the ACT to send the score that you like. This puts you in control of what the institute sees. Before the actual test, plan a nice trip somewhere to take with your child after the test. Your child will have something to look forward to after the real test is over.

LEAVING PUBLIC OR PRIVATE SCHOOL

Timing the day that your child leaves public or private school will require many considerations before making the final decision. Once your child is completely no longer academically challenged from the school, then you have a strong case to look into the possibility to see if your child could benefit from taking a college course. Before you pull your child out of school, consider the two possibilities for your child to stay in school.

1. You may have better luck getting your school to skip grades. Every time I have tried to get our child to skip grades, it was like going to the dentist and pulling teeth. One solution that was offered in California was for Chendara to take two classes with a class that was one grade above Chendara's.

2. Another possibility is for your child to audit a college course. This was made possible because the Bragg Elementary (local public) School's principal approved it. In addition, Cerritos College Admissions was more than willing to let Chendara take a class with

the opportunity to earn college credit. This situation will depend on the willingness of the local public school and the local college. Cerritos College allowed Chendara entrance at the age of eight. In California as well as here in Texas, I get this distinct felling that the local community colleges do not want to "steal" from the public schools. Whereas, allowing homeschoolers to audit isn't "stealing" from the public schools.

If an effort of the two does not work out, then pulling your child out of public school is a viable and necessary option. I officially home schooled my child when I make a declaration to the public school. We were fortunate to be self employed by the time our oldest was ready. This allowed us time to prepare her for college. I could schedule time to be off work to teach and prepare our children for college. Often, our children would work at our store and study at the same time. This period allowed me to prepare our child for the ACT test. Make sure that at least one of the parents could be a stay-at-home parent. Also make sure that the local college is willing to accept your child and your home school credentials without any prejudice of age.

HOME SCHOOL GRADUATION

Texas is a home school friendly state. Rules and regulations will vary from state to state. It was so easy; the only thing I did was inform the principal that I was going to be homeschooling. No forms to fill out, no credentials to obtain, no red tape, nothing. This was made possible by case law of Leeper vs. Arlington Independent School District on April 1987.

The Texas Home School Coalition (THSC) has been a great resource for me. Their web site is *www.thsc.org*. The THSC will help answer questions with

- ❖ GETTING STARTED
- ❖ CURRICULUM
- ❖ SCHOOL DISTRICT
- ❖ REQUIREMENTS
- ❖ HOMESCHOOLING TEENS

> Graduation requirement
> Diploma
> College entrance

According to THSC, "Home schools in Texas are private schools and not regulated by the state; therefore, home schools, just as with other private schools, set their own graduation standards. There is no minimum age requirement for graduation." This is the exact wording that I use on the transcript. Since I set my own standards, I decided when my kid is ready to graduate. Along with this are some measures that could be used. ACT is a good guide post to help determine a child's readiness. Depending on the state, each school has its own curriculum. Varying from school to school, not all Grade Point Averages (GPA) are created equally. The two main equalizers are the ACT or the SAT standardized tests.

Five out the six colleges that I have dealt with are child prodigy friendly. I believe that the experience nationwide comparatively has about the same proportion as my own personal experience. If a majority of college and universities are child prodigy friendly, then your child should have no problem with college entrance.

PART IV:

A Case for Child Prodigy

Does your child get good grades with little to no effort? Does your child get bored with school or homework? Then you might consider giving your child challenges that will lead him or her to become a child prodigy. When our first child was born, we didn't set out for her to be a child prodigy. In fact, all we wanted was for our children to have a normal life and do her best. Doing her best means continuing learning. The young mind has a window of opportunity. We never say, "that is good enough for their grade level." Instead, we ask, "Are they being challenged?" In Japan, there is a word call "Kaizen" which means continuous improvement. We take the Kaizen approach when it comes to our children's education.

There have been many struggles with trying to get the schools to keep our children challenged. Our goal is clear, keep the kids challenged. First we tried to get Chendara to skip Kindergarten. That didn't work out. Later in 2nd grade, we asked Chendara what she did in school. She replied—colored. We said that that was great! She responded, "I colored all day." When we inquired with the teacher, the teacher said, "that when Chendara was done very early with her assignment, I had her color the rest of the day." We were shocked. Needless to say, we didn't take things lying down. Which lead us to our final result, a child prodigy.

Q&A: CONCERNS ABOUT CHILD PRODIGY

The following are some common concerned questions that we get from other parents.

Question. I am expecting a child and am excited about raising a child prodigy, but I also have a toddler, and a teen, is it too late to start training?

Answer. No. I didn't start to read for pleasure until I was about 15. Although I was not a child prodigy myself, I did go on to earn my master's degree. It is never too late to instill the love of learning. Teach your child that learning can be fun and rewarding. The ultimate goal of raising a child prodigy isn't as important as the balance of mind, body, and spirit. No matter what age your child is, it is never too late. The portion in this book on college preparation and admission could be used for your child that is going to graduate high school at the "normal" age.

Another way to look at it is we ask ourselves, "is it too late to exercise and be fit?" Obviously it is never too late to take care of our bodies. Start at 40 or 50, we might not win any gold medals in the Olympics, but we will be better off for being fit and healthy. Start with the level your child is currently at, then develop the training to fit based on the general philosophies in this book.

Question. What about my kid's childhood? I don't know if my child will be ready for adult issues and subject matter?

Answer. We do our best not to rob Chendara and Marcie of their childhood. When you see them play with their relatives, church kids, and other children, you couldn't even tell that they are going to college. I honestly believe that we did a very good job at preserving their innocence.

In the best scenario, there would be a child prodigy college for minors only. Since there is no such college here locally, we do the best with what we have. Whether in an elementary classroom or college classroom, it is not a time to play but a time to learn. Outside the classrooms, there are plenty of play times at home, in the park, and on trips. And play they do.

Work is a great way to experience a piece of adulthood. Work ethics outside of the classrooms will transfer into work ethics in the classrooms. When it comes to work, we don't shelter our kids. The children in 3rd world counties and the pioneer children that traveled west were no strangers to work.

> *"Work Will Win When Wishy Washy Wishing Won't."*
>
> *Thomas S. Monson*

My wife has worked to help her family as long as she can remember. Since 12, I worked asphalt and roofing to support my Scouting habits. Our children were fortunate enough to help as servers at my sister's restaurant. Now we are fortunate that our kids could help us with running the register and stocking at our gas station business. Many times parents want their child to have a better life than they had. Unfortunately, this includes the pleasure of not having to work. Work is not wasted energy; rather, work is a gift. Work is a gift that needs to be passed on to our children. In a wonderful book (and movie), *The Ultimate Gift*, by Jim Stovall, "I learned the satisfaction that comes from a simple four-letter word: work. One of the things my wealth has robbed from you and the entire family is the privilege and satisfaction that comes from doing an honest day's work."[9] I believe that work starts at a young age and then transitions into classroom and adulthood.

It helps by having an open conversation with our kids about adult related issues. Every child matures at a different age. By the time Chendara entered college at age 13, she was very mature when it came to adult subjects. She had no problems dealing with adult content subject matter. There was a legitimate concern when Marcie was nine while attending Cossatot Community College. Marcie's Developmental Writing teacher, Sheri Hodges, recommended some great books for her to read before she took Freshman Composition. She has a passion for reading teen chapter books and mysteries. We had Marcie switch back and forth between the books that she loves and the recommended books by her college instructor. I remember her first assigned book when she came and said, "Daddy, on page 10 it has the F word." That is when I had to explain to her that sometimes college textbooks feel it necessary to use profanity. Also some adults use it quite often. She has adapted really well in her comprehension and is good about coming to my wife and me to help her expand on a certain subject. The teacher's recommendation tremendously helped Marcie prepare for Freshman Composition to deal with subject matter along with her adult counterparts.

Question. How will the adults in college treat my child?

Answer. Respect is something that is earned at any given age. The fact that your child had to work his way to be at college level has already earned a certain amount of respect. When a child prodigy child enters college with humility and maturity, adults will automatically respect that. No one likes a "know it all." So remember that humility and maturity will gain respect. When in Rome, act as a Roman. When in college, act as an adult. There will be plenty of play time off campus.

Not only will the adult students be nice, they will also offer insights into the adult world. This is especially true for evening classes where there tends to be more working adults that attend college after a long day's work. Some of these adults have hit the corporate ceiling and need more education to help break the glass ceiling. Others just want to entirely change their careers. Listening to real life stories directly from adults will have a strong impact on your child prodigy. Divorce, bankruptcy, addiction, parenting, and work are some of the life lessons that are priceless to learn as a youth. Many of these adults are more than willing to help your child prodigy avoid the same mistakes they have made. As parents, we could talk until we are blue in the face and will not have the same amount of influence as if it came from another adult.

Question. I know that my child is not being challenged at school right now, but will he be able to handle college level work?

Answer. Absolutely. If your child meets the college's admission requirements, then he is ready for college level work. Colleges do their best at screening to make sure that the students are qualified. When students drop-out, that hurts the school's retention rate.

Community colleges have placement tests for their students. Let's face it, not all high school students that graduate high school are ready for college level work. Students need to pass the reading, writing, and arithmetic portion of the placement test. There are developmental classes for students that do not pass part or the entire placement test. For example, if the student passes the reading and writing and not the math; then the student may take Pre-Algebra while taking other college courses. ACT and SAT are great equalizers since not all GPAs (Grade Point Average) are created equal across the country.

You can feel confident that as you prepare your child to meet the ACT standards, he will be more than prepared. When Cossatot Community College saw Chendara's ACT score, they knew that she would have no problem. CCCUA was also kind enough to give Marcie a placement test. The placement test correctly showed what developmental classes Marcie needed. These tests are well designed to correctly place a student in the right class.

Question. I only have a high school diploma and that was many years ago. Will I have the "know how" to teach a child prodigy?

Answer. Yes, no problem, you are fine. This book was designed just for you. It is not a thesis for a PhD. The main thing that is required from you as a parent is the strong desire and 99% perspiration on your part. I hope that this book is easy to comprehend and that the principles are simple and straight forward.

My wife has a high school diploma and some college. She came to America not speaking a word of English at the age of 12, yet she did and continues to do the majority of the teaching when it comes to reading and writing to all of our children.

> *"Teach your children well...feed them on your dreams...just look at them and sigh, and know they love you."*
>
> *Crosby, Stills, Nash, and Young*

Remember, you are preparing your child to attend college, not trying to be their college professor. He or she only has to be at the 12th grade level. Currently, Marcie is taking Calculus II, and I have no clue what she is doing in that class. She is passing the class with the help from the tutor lab and her fellow classmates.

There is great joy for a Kung Fu Master when his disciple exceeds his skills. A Kung Fu student truly honors his master when he has accomplish all the training his master has to offer and goes beyond with greater strength, speed, agility, and technique. Imagine how great your joy will be when your child is the first in the family to graduate from college or even earn a doctorate!

Question. Will I have enough time to train a child prodigy because I don't want to spend from Sun up to Sun down?

Answer. This is not a 24/7 non-stop cramming program. Remember fun and rest. As a trainer, you will spend more time as a guide. You're the coach on the bicycle while the athlete is running or jogging.

IN CHENDARA'S WORDS

When I was eight, I had a great chance to watch the movie *Legally Blonde.* Sounds really dumb, but it's true. And a little eight year old can be easily persuaded and thoughts can be changed really fast. Well that movie made me want to go to college or a university just like Ell Woods did. I told my parents what I wanted. Unlike many parents, my parents actually took it seriously. They started looking at the local college and the classes that would be available to me. They took an even bigger step and actually enrolled me in college. Along the way, they fought plenty of people who felt the need to oppose this opportunity that I had. I took a 3 credit Basic Math class and received a B+. That one class helped me all the way through my public school years. I didn't learn anything new in the subject of math all through and until 7th grade because that one class taught me so many things that kids my age wouldn't have learned until years later.

Well, as the years passed and I went on with normal school, I felt like I wasn't really that challenged. The homework was too easy or I felt it was pointless because I knew that I could be learning something new instead of the same thing each year so I just slacked off. So the solution my parents came up with was to put me in college full time so I can reach the potential that I had. I'm not going to lie; I did have a little bit of a hard time adjusting. But it's not for the reason that everyone thinks.

I have always felt that my age didn't really reflect who I really was and how I thought. I didn't really have any trouble getting along with people that are twice or triple my age. That is the concern that I have heard the most. My adult peers really do help me tremendously. My past classmates have definitely been there to lead me into the right direction and gave me their wisdom about the class and even life. I have learned an amazing number of things by being around real people. And when I mean real, I mean people that have gone through things like divorce, marriage, financial trouble, family issues, and many different trials and aspects of life. I have learned so much from these great people. Being with adult peers and along with working at my parents store absolutely matured me by an amazing amount. Actually, when I get to hang around kids my age I feel slightly awkward. If you don't fit into their "world," then you're just weird, and they feel like they have every right to degrade you. I feel that I am on a whole different level than the kids my age are, and those who are around me can feel that. There is a sense of respect towards me from my fellow teens. The issue that plenty of people have about "educationally ready but not maturely ready" makes me upset in a way. Even though I was already somewhat mature before going into college, it was because I went to college that I am who I am today.

I understand that parents want to protect their kids from harm and that is another reason why they wouldn't want their kids in college full of adults. Yes there are bad people out there, but there are good ones, too. I personally feel on this issue that you can't protect your child from everything. If it happens, it happens. Someone might kidnap your child at the park even right in front of you, so does that mean you don't allow your child to go to the park anymore? Some person could physically hurt or harm your child at church, so does that mean you don't allow him or her to go to church anymore? Now I absolutely hope and pray that this does not happen to anybody's child. But in this world, about any bad thing can happen anywhere at any time. But that does not mean that you shun everything and lock yourself away. I mean, your child could be harmed at the very learning center they are in now.

I had sort of a hard time adjusting to the "losing childhood" issue. I did fight the idea that I would have to leave my friends and not get to see them everyday like I used to. This really depends on the parents. I can see it is an issue, if the parents won't let their kid see their friends at all for whatever reason or not talk to them. It is completely up to how the parents raise their child. But going to college is definitely worth it in the long run. And if you get to see your friends that are your age while you are attending college then it will be so much fun. Going to college at a young age has benefited me, my future spouse and children, my family, and all those around me.

For me, I am glad that I had this opportunity to pursue my dream of becoming a restaurant owner with educational advantage. I know if I had gone on to high school that I wouldn't have reached my full potential. Yeah, I miss that I could have been on the volleyball team, having a go at trying to be prom queen, talk about who everyone's crushing on, and all that good teenage stuff. But I wouldn't be the person who I am today and I feel satisfied with myself and wouldn't change my personality for anyone else's. Well, maybe Mariah Carey. Haha . . . just kidding! Even with some of my human nature glitches, I still love who and what I am. And who knows . . . maybe someone might take me to prom! I'm crossing my fingers.

IN MARCIE'S WORDS

I enjoy going to Texas A&M—Texarkana. The campus is new and everyone is friendly. Everyone is always helpful. There are many clubs and organizations at the campus. The Multicultural Association (MCA), Campus Activities Board (CAB), the biology club, future teachers association, and the history club are just a few of the many clubs that are at A&M-Texarkana. I am in MCA and CAB committee. I am very involved in the two clubs and go to just about every meeting and event. I am glad that they treat me like any other students and not an eleven year old.

There is one place that I go to almost every day. That is the Academic Skills and Knowledge (ASK) center. I go there before, between, and after my classes. The tutors there are very helpful. The one on one tutoring at the ASK center is free. I tutor College Algebra part-time at the ASK center.

Since I am not old enough to work, I volunteer. I don't mind not getting paid to tutor because it keeps my math skills sharp. All of the students appreciate my help and don't feel intimidated by an eleven year old.

Overall, I have a lot of fun at the University. The students, professors, and staffs are really nice to me. I get use the school's discount card along with my student I.D. to get discounts around town. Last semester I got straight "A" with 12 units. This semester I am taking 15 units. I look forward to graduating with all of my freshmen friends in the year 2014.

IN MARTHA'S WORDS

Ramon, Martha's dad, works at our gas station. I helped counsel and advise Ramon in regard to the idea of the child prodigy. Martha took a full semester at CCCUA. Later at age 15, she was a full-time student at Texas A&M University-Texarkana. Here's Martha:

Starting college at an early age was an important step for my future. I felt that public school was limiting my intellectual capacity. Since an early age, I felt the drive to succeed in my studies. As I grew older, the homework given to me was not challenging enough. Therefore, I made the difficult decision of finishing high school through home school. Soon after that, I began my first college courses at the age of 15. Many teenagers my age find high school a great social experience, but I feel it does not prepare you for the real world. Since I am expected to be responsible for my own work, college has made me mature faster. The college "experience" is an opportunity I recommend to teenagers my age, but you must have the desire to learn. I also appreciate all the help that I have received from Jet. Without him guiding me through the steps of entering college, I would not be where I am today.

BENEFITS IN A NUT SHELL

In our quest for Kaizen's continuous improvement for our children, we have noticed certain benefits:

- **Five Minutes of Fame**—Being in the newspapers and TV has boosted the egos. The girls and I enjoy it.
- **Economic**—Going to school while still living at home saves money from dorms and living expense. Graduating college at a younger age gives the child prodigy better chance at to good paying job.
- **Adult Association**—Being around adult students helps the child prodigy get an adult perspective.
- **Early Start in Life**—Getting an early start gives you a heads up in life—financially and academically.
- **Planning Skills**—Setting goals with the degree plan from the college helps the child prodigy become better at planning and setting goals in other aspects of their lives.
- **Challenging Academics**—Avoiding boredom is always a plus.
- **Life-Long Love for Learning**—Learning because you want to and not because you have to is a great blessing.

CONCLUSION

It is my hope and dream that child prodigies become more of the norm and not the exception. Young people today have the potential to achieve great things for themselves and our society. I have all the confidence in the youth of today. Furthermore, I believe that the next generation will be known as one of the Greatest Generations that will restore the constitution to the way our founding fathers envisioned it to be. Today, the opportunities, technologies, and responsibilities are the greatest. Imagine young minds going on to find the cure for cancer, discover new medicine, find new ways to travel space, solve many riddles of the universe, and make this world a better place. It can happen and it will happen if we help invest in our most precious commodity, our children.

I believe that the blue print of the philosophies that I have laid out for raising child prodigy is simple and common sense. A simple and common sense blue print of losing weight is diet and exercise; going to the gym and not eating as much food as we want is not so easy. The counsel we get for our pastor, reverend, bishop, priest, father, monk, and other church leaders are simple; choosing to follow them is another matter. I said the philosophies contained in this book were simple, not easy. Will training your child to be a prodigy child be easy? NO. However, will it be worth it? YES, and a thousand more times YES. You can do it. I believe that anyone with a high school education, or less, can help his or her child excel in education.

There are plenty of resources to help us develop our children. The responsibilities will always be ours as parents, no matter how many resources there are or we lack thereof. We should not feel entitled from public

> *"Train up a child in the way he should go: and when he is old, he will not depart from it."*
>
> *Proverbs 22:6*

schools, churches, or the society to educate our child. Raising your child to be a child prodigy will take great effort and a good amount of sacrifice by forgoing some self-interest and personal desires and goals. However, it is worth it as you dedicate your time, money, and energy to the greatest commodity on earth, our children.

As your child becomes more educated, teach them to be humble. Remember that learning is not wisdom. There are plenty of smart people that do stupid and unethical things. Our world needs more intellectual and spiritual

> "O that cunning plan of the evil one! O the vainness, and the frailties, and the foolishness of men! When they are learned they think they are wise, and they hearken not unto the counsel of God, for they set it aside, supposing they know of themselves, wherefore, their wisdom is foolishness and it profiteth them not. And they shall perish. But to be learned is good if they hearken unto the counsels of GOD.
> 2 Nephi 9: 28&29

people. Children need a good balance of physical, spiritual, and moral health. The United States of America is truly a blessed land with many opportunities.

It has been a wonderful journey so far for our two child prodigies, my wife, and me. May you have a fantastic experience as you train your precious child to be a child prodigy. In this complex and competitive society, may your child prodigy use their education to improve their lives and the lives of their fellow humankind. God bless.

NOTES

Scripture quotations of the *Old Testament* and *New Testament* have been taken from the King James Version. Scripture quotations of the *Book of Mormon, Another Testament of Jesus Christ* is published by The Church of Jesus Christ of Latter-day Saints.

1. Hinckley, Gordon B. "Words of the Prophet: Seek Learning." *<http://www.lds.org/ldsorg/v/index.jsp?hideNav=1&locale=0&sourc eId=8ebf742e3547411 0VgnVCM100000176f620a____&vgnext oid=024644f8f206c010VgnVCM1000004d82620aRCRD>*

2. Levin, Mark. *Liberty and Tyranny*. New York, New York: Threshold Editions, 2009.

3. Eyring, Henry. *Reflections of a Scientist*. Salt Lake City, Utah: Deseret Book, 1983

4. Stafford, Michelle. *Raising a Child Prodigy. <http://ezinearticles. com/?Raising-a-Child-Prodigy&id=1743358>*.

5. Levin, Mark. *Liberty and Tyranny*. New York, New York: Threshold Editions, 2009

6. *Home Schooling Outstanding Results National Tests*. Washington Times. *<http://www.washingtontimes.com/news/2009/aug/30/ home-schooling-outstanding-results-national-tests/>* August 30, 2009.

7. My result from the Los Angeles Marathon in 2004. *<http://www. athlinks.com/myresults.aspx?rid=6164394>*.

8. Galloway, Jeff *Jeff Galloway's Book on Running.* Bolinas: Shelter Publications, 2002

9. Stovall, Jim. *The Ultimate Give.* Publisher: David C. Cook, 2001

APPENDIX A

 Cossatot
COMMUNITY COLLEGE
UNIVERSITY OF ARKANSAS

ASSOCIATE OF ARTS DEGREE FAST TRACK
AAFT: 63-65 Hrs.
Updated 8-6-10

This plan is designed for those students who have the required placement scores to begin college level work. It is fast paced, so please make sure you have the necessary time and organizational skills to complete this program.

To qualify for the fast track transfer degree plan, the student must meet ALL of the following requirements: High School Diploma or GED; ACT scores of 19 or above in Math English, Reading; or COMPASS Scores of at least 41 in Algebra, 75 in Writing, and 82 in Reading.

This degree will provide the student with an Associate of Arts degree. It is the responsibility of the student to contact and work with the transfer institution regarding the degree requirements for its 4-year program. The courses do not have to be taken in the semester listed except for the Orientation and the Composition classes, but the number of credit hours must be maintained. Further the college guarantees that the courses will be offered, but not the mode of delivery or the campus site

Completed	Area / Course Number	Course Title (& options)
	Summer (June – July) 13 HRS.	
	SPD 1101	Fast Track Orientation
	ENGL 1113	Composition I (June 4-week term)
	MATH 1023	College Algebra
	ENGL 1123	Composition II (July-4 week term)
	Elective (3 hrs.)	
	Fall (August – December) 19 HRS	
	ENGL 2213	World Literature to 1650
	HIST 2013	US History to 1876 **OR**
	HIST 2023	US History since 1876
	BIOL	Biological Science Requirement
	FA 2003	Introduction to Fine Arts – Art **OR**
	FA 2013	Introduction to Fine Arts – Music
	SPCH 1113	Principles of Speech
	Elective (3 hours)	
	Spring (January - May) 17 hrs.	
	ENGL 2223	World Literature since 1650
	BIOL, CHEM, GEOL, ASTR	Physical Science Requirement
	HIST 1003	Western Civilization to 1700 **OR**
	HIST 1013	Western Civilization Since 1700
	PHED	Physical Education Requirement
	Social Science Elective	From ECON, HIST, PSYC, SOC, PSCI, GEOG (other than used above)
	Elective (3 hours)	
	Summer (June - July) 12 hrs	
	PSCI 2003	American Government
	HS 1403	Personal & Community Health
	Social Science Elective	From ECON, HIST, PSYC, SOC, PSCI, GEOG (other than used above)
	Elective (3 hours)	

June 16, 2010

Age bias case: Is 13 too young for community college?

By David Moltz, *Inside Higher Ed*

Anastasia Megan, a 13-year-old Florida girl who has nearly completed her high-school curriculum via homeschooling, tried to take dual-enrollment courses at Lake-Sumter Community College last year. She was denied entry, however, by administrators who thought she was not ready to sit alongside older students in the classroom. The Education Department's Office for Civil Rights is now investigating whether the decision violated anti-bias law—raising an issue that comes up at other community colleges as well.

The Age Discrimination Act of 1975 "prohibits discrimination on the basis of age in programs and activities receiving federal financial assistance." Arguing that Lake-Sumter violated this law, Megan's parents filed a complaint in December. Federal law requires mediation attempts for age-discrimination complaints like this one; Education Department officials confirm that mediation failed in the Lake-Sumter case and that the matter is now under investigation by the Office for Civil Rights.

Megan and her parents could not be reached for comment. Her parents have said in past interviews, however, that sending their daughter to any other institution would involve moving the entire family. They noted, too, that they are not interested in enrolling her in online courses. "If she meets all the qualifications but for her age, then why not let her in?" Louise Racine, Megan's mother, told the Orlando Sentinel last month. "What's the worst that can happen, honestly? If a child does pass these tests, don't you think they should be allowed to continue their education to the next level and continue to let their minds grow?"

PHOTO GALLERY: Anastasia Megan, too young at 13?
ON THE WEB: Easing the transition from high school
MORE FROM INSIDE HIGHER ED: Dual degree for a different high school population

When Megan was denied entry to Lake-Sumter last fall, there was no formal rule stipulating that applicants be of a certain age to gain admission. Charles Mojock, president at Lake-Sumter, told Inside Higher Ed that the college has long had an informal minimum age requirement of 15 but that a rule was only drafted following Megan's complaint. In April, the college's Board of Trustees unanimously approved a change to its rules stating that the college "accepts all students who have reached the age of fifteen (15) years on or before the first day of classes each term" and have either earned a high school diploma, a General Equivalency Diploma, previously completed college-level work or completed a home-school program. There is a clause in the rule change that allows for the president to grant exceptions.

Though Mojock would not discuss the Megan complaint specifically, he defended his college's age restriction for students, saying he believes "the rule is fair and reasonable" and has "enough flexibility" so that it can be appealed and overturned in extenuating circumstances.

"You can be the best driver in the world at age 12, but you can't get a driver's license," said Mojock. "You can also vote at 18, but does that 18-year-old always know what he or she's talking about? That's not always the case. We're trying to be accommodating, and every occasion is a different endeavor. Still, we accept that age is a placeholder for certain readiness in a number of other areas in our society. I don't see how this is out of the question. We're not being arbitrary."

Mojock noted that the college considers "experience" and "relative maturity" when considered whether to let in someone younger than 15 years old. Though he acknowledged that he rarely grants waivers to this rule, he admitted the college has accepted younger students in the past. For example, the college's commencement speaker this year was a 16-year-old graduate who started taking dual-enrollment courses when she was 14 years old.

By and large, Mojock argued, a 15-year-old student is better qualified for the college environment than someone two years younger, because he or she has probably had more interaction with those of a traditional college age. For those younger than 15, Mojock said he worries about issues of "safety and security" on his campus, given that it is open to the entire community and not as strictly guarded as a high school campus.

Open doors

The idea of very young college students is hardly limited to Doogie Howser, M.D. Mary Baldwin College's Program for the Exceptionally Gifted and Simon's Rock of Bard College are two different approaches to reaching students well before a traditional high school graduation. But for community colleges, which do not have specifically designed programs, the prospect of a 13-year-old on campus may raise different issues. It is not clear how many such students there are, but some believe they are on the rise. Education department data show that from 2003 to 2007 the percentage of community college students age 18 and under grew from 5.3% to 6.7%—not including students who are dual-enrolled in community college courses while in high school—but most of these students are likely 17—and 18-year-old students.

Not all younger students, however, are turned away. Last month, Chendara Tiraphatna, a 15-year-old girl, became the youngest graduate of Cossatot Community College of the University of Arkansas—an institution that had no problem admitting her at age 13 to its associate of arts fast track program.

Tiraphatna, the daughter of immigrants from Thailand and Cambodia, withdrew from her middle school, near the state-straddling city of Texarkana, in 2008. She said she simply was not challenged enough by the coursework, so her parents started homeschooling her after the 7th grade.

"It just got to the point where we couldn't handle it anymore," said Jittakron "Jet" Tiraphatna, Chendara's father, of homeschooling her. "She was already at the college level."

Jet worked with nearby Texarkana College, a community college that allowed Chendara to audit a few courses while she was being homeschooled. Still, when Chendara eventually tried to seek full-time admission to the college, she was denied because of her age.

A Texarkana College spokeswoman explained that the institution's admissions policies stipulate that students who are not graduates of state-accredited high schools cannot be considered for admission until age 18. At the same time, the college's updated course catalog notes that "It is the policy of Texarkana College to admit students without regard to race, color, sex, disability, age, or national origin." Specific stipulations of policy also permit early admission for students who complete the 10th grade and have the consent of their parents and the recommendation of their high school principal.

"It's a shame that a school would turn down a child simply based on age," Jet Tiraphatna said. "Each child is different. I see some 11-year-olds that I'd put up against an 18-year-old any day. (Chendara) is an adult and she can handle it. No school should have the right to say, based on your age, that you cannot attend. There should be the right to give every kid an opportunity to prove him—or herself."

Having been denied admission to Texarkana Community College, Chendara sought admission at another two-year institution, just across the state line in Arkansas: Cossatot Community College. This time, after she proved her college readiness through a series of tests, there were no further questions.

"That was pretty much it," wrote Mark Riley, spokesman at Cossatot, in an e-mail. "They came to us and we said, 'Sure, we'll enroll you.' We didn't bend any rules just so we could score a (public relations) coup. We admitted her because she met our requirements for admission."

Chendara said she was treated like just another student by her professors and fellow students at Cossatot. Having audited a few community college courses prior to her full-time enrollment, she said, she was more than ready to start and fit in.

"I've heard some people say, 'She might be educationally ready but she might not be mature enough,'" Chendara explained. "I get really upset with that. Sometimes I feel like I have a higher maturity level than some of the students I'm with in class. If you're educationally ready and you want it, why not? Age is just a number, and people mature at different rates."

Chendara also takes issue with the argument that her being so young presents a safety or security risk for her on campus.

"You can only protect yourself for so long," Chendara said. "I've actually had a lot of older guys ask me out and hit on me and stuff. I've prepared myself, and I say that I'm only 15. You just have to use common sense. I hope most people have that. I mean, there are people looking out for me. My parents drop me off and pick me up after school and ask if everything was OK. Also, my professors keep an eye out for me."

Though Chendara is already on track to earn her baccalaureate degree in business administration from Texas A&M at Texarkana, she is in many ways typical of someone her age: she said she is actively studying and "so psyched" to earn her driver's license next year, and she and her father are currently arguing over whether or not she should be allowed to attend the prom at a local high school. All things considered, she said she feels like a normal teenager.

"I don't think I've lost my childhood," Chendara said. "I enjoy the life I have now. I have friends and I hang out with them all the time. They understand me and don't treat me any differently."

The legal debate

Christine Helwick, general counsel for the California State University system, said the issue of whether a college has the right to bar a student from admission based on age has not been tested in court of by the federal government. She acknowledged that the OCR case involving Lake-Sumter may be the first opportunity for one of these bodies to apply a legal standard.

"The questions are all contextual," Helwick explained. "I can imagine lots of arguments that a college would make as to why this is not age discrimination. Whether any of those would carry the day, I don't know."

Nancy Tribbensee, general counsel for the Arizona Board of Regents, said, prior to reading about the Lake-Sumter case, she was not aware that any institutions were imposing an age requirement.

"If a college approached me about this, I'd make it more of a conversation about common sense," Tribbensee said. "Given that their campuses are open, I would ask how being a student poses a greater risk. If there is a danger for kids on campus, there are likely already kids out there on campus who aren't students. If you're concerned about students' level of maturity, that's a dangerous road. The students you admit already encompass a wide maturity level. I would just tick through these reasons. There are ways to limit each of these concerns in a way that would stop short of enforcing an age restriction."

Still, Tribbensee said there are some cases where an age-restriction might make sense. For example, she noted that courses about making wine or beer brewing are often restricted to those who are at least 21, given that students cannot participate in class tastings if they are not of age.

APPENDIX C

Letter of Recommendation for Honor's Scholarship from Instructor Karen Arbuckle

Dear Colleagues:

I am happy to write a letter of recommendation for Chendara Tiraphatna in support of her application for an Honor's Scholarship at Texas A & M. Ms. Tiraphatna has successfully taken my biology class and my anatomy/physiology class. Based on her performance in these courses, I strongly recommend her as the recipient of this award.

I have been acquainted with Ms. Tiraphatna for several semesters in my capacity as a teacher at Cossatot Community College of the University of Arkansas. Ms. Tiraphatna is efficient, competent and has an excellent rapport with people of all ages. Her communication skills, both written and verbal, are well developed. Based on her grades, attendance and class participation, I'd rate her academic performance in my class as one of the most exceptional students I've had the honor of instructing. It is especially noteworthy to mention her attitude towards class work. More than once I've seen older, more experienced students falter at the large amount of coursework involved in our Anatomy & Physiology class; however, Ms. Tiraphatna never flinched and completed all course material consistently and accurately.

Ms. Tiraphatna's performance on the Biology lecture exams demonstrates that she is disciplined in her studies and has the understanding required to grasp the material that accompanies a class as demanding as college biology. She has also demonstrated that she excels in group lab work as well as her individual studies.

I am sure that Ms. Tiraphatna will continue to succeed in her studies. She is a dedicated student, and her grades have been consistently exemplary. She always shows great initiative and diligence and her attitude is very pleasant and encouraging.

Please feel free to call [phone number and email omitted] if I can be of further help.

Sincerely,

Karen Arbuckle
Instructor of Biological Sciences
Cossatot Community College of the University of Arkansas

ABOUT THE AUTHOR

Jittakorn "JET" Tiraphatna and his wife Chenda had five children. The oldest, Chendara received her Associates Degree from Cossatot Community College at the age of 15 and is working on her Bachelor in Business at Texas A&M—Texarkana. Marcie was a full-time freshman at Texas A&M—Texarkana at age 10. Her first class at A&M was Calculus. Robert, Jacob, and Jared are currently enrolled in a local elementary school.

Jet is an Eagle Scout. Training boys has been a pleasure while serving as scoutmaster for many years. Serving as young men's president (youth ministry), his duties include overseeing the entire youth program from 2-18 years old when he served as a councilor in the bishopric (assistant pastor). Professionally, Jet worked for Learning for Life. He has been district executive, district director, and marketing director when he worked for the Boy Scouts of America.

Jet emigrated from Thailand to America at the age of 6 without knowing a single word of English. He overcame his "slow learning" and criticism from teachers and relatives to earn a Masters in Business Administration (MBA). He applied strong work ethic and sheer determination to balance between his employment, family, church duties, and college. Over the years, he has developed some learning and teaching philosophies. Applying these philosophies has generated great results with his children.

Edwards Brothers, Inc.
Thorofare, NJ USA
July 27, 2011